I0530290

RADIANT
WOUND

POEMS BY
CARA WATERFALL

UNSOLICITED
PRESS
PORTLAND, OREGON
SINCE 2012

For information contact:

Unsolicited Press

Portland, Oregon

www.unsolicitedpress.com

orders@unsolicitedpress.com

619-354-8005

Cover Design: Kathryn Gerhardt

Editor: Summer Stewart

ISBN: 978-1-963115-77-2

POEMS

I

OXYGEN AWAKENS A FLAME

ABIDJAN AUBADE

Roadside,
doleful icons
glisten, listening
in the penumbra
of green
tarpaulins

A Madonna beseeches,
swaddled in blue,
eight pale replicas
at her feet, bleached
folds of taffeta flecked
with soot

Men crouch
on a strip
of cracked tarmac,
palms touching mat,
as bats slouch
toward the city
in the close-mouthed
dawn

The cathedral looms,
entreats the lagoon

with a quaver
of prayers,
its concrete regalia
made radiant
by morning

In silken pews,
women fan faces,
bright as July,
as their lips
assail psalms
an octave below
a siren's wail,
each syllable
swabbing
the stained glass
clean

Waking rituals
array the day
with elaborate intention
until the unshackled sun
makes a wreck of them
and they melt
into morning's bright

                    unrest

ODE TO THE COCKROACH

Ferrous body, feral heart, you were forged elsewhere — alloy of alien parts: the brassy husk, barbed limbs. Form built for velocity, fiery wings throttle air, compel those swift stems of liquorice to feast on stamp glue, peppermint wrappers, bits of lint. At dusk, you declare regency over each room. A blade of light cleaves the gloom momentarily You are reborn at night, you glow auburn, glower. Those prehistoric eyes prowl this hive, divining the embryonic to the refined. Creature without coda or quota. Like dark matter, everywhere unseen & everywhere in between. You combat lessening with glut, a brew of genetics & good luck, bend the world to your bias, & — like a virus —   always keen to reinvent. If called for, your belly embraces deprivation. Adaptation is your birthright — to outlive, outlast. Something encoded in the brain convulses with closure; corrodes restraint, compels you closer to the carnal. (Procreate & you may replicate something of the eternal.) Kinetic with intent, you tear into the hereafter, bold beneath the aegis, the armour of grit & sinew. You understand as we do: time is carnivorous.

SIMULACRUM

We breathe in diesel & dust,
the plane's moan a distant souvenir,
the highway mimicking
my mouth's hard line.

An elegy spins its wheels
in my head, for the city
we left behind.

The dream of sleep rises
in black peaks,
the swarm of miles
receding.

As our car speeds over the bridge,
the lagoon, a shineless expanse
like pavement, painted
by the same swelter.

A bat looms, so tiny
in the enormous night,
hollow with longing.
& like that, time widens

& I am cleaving the clouds,
peeling wisp upon wisp
from my eyes until
I am hovering above

the flawless slick of highways,
beaded with road studs,
& flanked by buildings
in postures of abandonment —

the streetlamps bent
as a goat's hind legs,
their light
skinned of softness,

a vacant shrine illuminated
by the moon, its statue
dragged from its perch.

Crows swell around the pedestal.
They form a revenant,
a wakeful thing, its soul
at last remembered.

ATELIER

Zone 4, Abidjan, Côte d'Ivoire

A house huddles in the dank hush
of a shade-flattened glade,
its rafters dark as charred fish.

Blackened stones make a path to the back
where a roof buckles
over vertices of stacked tables.

Its eaves teeter
with putrid leaves
& caravans of ants.

Cankered chairs sag in wood chips,
wads of cardboard, trampled *Awa* bottles.
Doors scab in the swelter.

A strand of rattan lanterns ripens into cauls
of mould. The sun embers
a bedspring.

Cracks cobweb the vinyl of a sofa.
Beetles tenant the cadaver
of a mannequin.

Lime-washed by time, twelve lamp-bases line up
like apostles, plugs coiled
like chokers.

And a ladder of drawers is a monument
to the silverfish
slinking within it.

Rehearsing for the metamorphosis,
the fretwork fills
with salvaged light.

A miniature amphitheatre with micro-
elegies everywhere, each
awaiting a saviour.

THE CHICKEN CARVER

atelier in Zone 4, Abidjan, Côte d'Ivoire

dawn saws through   a scrapyard   where a lanky man sits
legs akimbo   hemmed in by two-limbed stools   & helices
of cedar   stonewashed jeans saddled in shavings   scalp leashed
by dust   ants chafe his ankles   as the mosquito coil   clots
with sawdust   a transistor radio   buzzes   on its back
bent antenna broadcasting   the chaos   of static & ash
he is mining the wood   hatching lines   slivers   drip   with
every *scritch-scritch*   of the chisel   each scratch   as
thin   as a stitch   he threshes   a tremor of feathers   & shirrs
the fleecy chest   gouges the lithe hollow   of the throat
scissors away a beak   & smooths it   with a rasp   & its torso
ebbs   into pedestalled claws   they roost in pairs   corseted
in scores   he fishes another   wooden block   from the singed
underbrush   spent firewood   his hands   shudder   with
the held lament   of decades of work   when he rises
feet disheveling dirt   spine limp   as a marionette's
his shadow drops   into the deadfall   a   tree   holds
the   balding moon   in its burnt   fingers   as he
disappears   a plume   of smoke

ODE TO RUST

Helicopter at Aburi Botanical Gardens, near Accra, Ghana

oxygen awakens a flame
lays bare your ashen ligaments,
your estranged ancestry

the bombast of locust
weaves through your chassis
tasting blood
in furred mazes

a receptacle flush with myth,
your freckled bones speak of
burnished bullets, blistered gussets,
battalions of rot

a palimpsest of chrome
and clouds of moss,
your metal seems immortal,
but is made flesh by air

dusk's cavalry of light
kindles the wrinkled bronze

of your blades, ignites your patina
a corrosive rose

your cockpit is a riven cranium
its jaws sutured by wire,
its tail boom dislocated,
rudder bent like a knee in the dirt

an unclaimed headstone
under the cupola of trees,
vanished men
                    mere emblem

FOUR ASPECTS OF LANGUAGE [A SEA LIVES ON MY TONGUE]

A sea lives on my tongue,
a whale-fall, ponderous
as a herd of rocks, churning
dark infinities of water,
sharpening its tired lustre.

//

From root to crown, sap
flows around, trapping me
in its cloying braid. A forest
lives on my tongue,
its chorus glottal & chopped.

//

Silence writhes like a lizard
in a hyena's maw. An island lives
on my tongue, its sound
fissured, a cadaver
dyeing the blank sands red.

//

Where birds, pale as granite,
hang in effigy, night's quiet
flaking like mica from their bodies.
A mountain lives on my tongue.

SELF-PORTRAIT AS ROUNDABOUT MANNEQUIN

Riviera Golf, Abidjan

I am crude in the daylight,
a sepulchral figure
cloaked in khaki dust,
my mouth swilling
city grit as dirt pinwheels
through the ribs
of an iron bedframe.

By afternoon,
my shadow falls
twice as long.

At night,
vampiric in the moonlight,
my jaundiced skin glistens.
Headlights crisscross
each shellacked follicle
& the puckered sheen
of my brain.

//

Rain dribbles into the crater
where my left eye
once nested & gutters out,
rinses the grubby indent of my navel
& gravel-dented calves.

Looted by the elements,
sometimes a body fits
amid the bric-a-brac
but nowhere else.

//

At rush hour,
I parse the landscape:
each yellowing shirt & stiff skirt,
every motor roaring
through my hollowed torso,
every rubbernecker —

                    or is there nobody?

Am I nobody
                    amid the din?

//

Newness has its own

bittersweet pathology.

I am made of skin & seam
& apprehension.

But my heart has heft,
still blooms under this ruptured blue,
aches in the electric air.

Stuck in this outdoor pew,
a love story could unfold.

//

The sun sets
through my absent eye.
I glow, radiant
as any wound.
-

UNSOLICITED
PRESS
PORTLAND, OREGON
EST. 2012

II

RED CANVAS

UNSOLICITED
PRESS
PORTLAND, OREGON
EST 2012

UNSOLICITED
PRESS
PORTLAND, OREGON

RED CANVAS

Bingerville, Cote d'Ivoire

*"I was painting and blood spattered onto my canvas. A bullet had
grazed a woman who was running with her child. I left the
wound to say 'never again.'"*
*~ Yubah Sanogo, about the 2010-2011
post-electoral crisis*

I see red / in the forecast / a crimson dye spreading
across the sky / punctured by gunfire
& the hiss of smoke

I see a wound in the sky / rubricating the clouds
as the bazaar of war / saturates
my city red

I see the entrails / of dead chickens auguring
men / wet with sweat / & women
flesh drenched red

I see the penumbra / of carrion beetles underfoot
as they swim / toward the pulp
of red bodies

I see fear tunnel / into faces / through the round caves
of eyes / the reckless mouths
the red garb of the body

I see the bedlam of a red city / its burning cutbanks
its bloody corona / & the red clamour
of the rooster / on the roof

I see blue men / running / with white masks
bearing red bodies / in black tarps

I cannot unsee / these colours
this timbre of red / this rhythm of light

the canvas speaks

      my paintbrush writes

LE PRÉSIDENT: SEVEN DAYS

In the beginning, Le Président, flattened his ancestral village[1], to create his idea of heaven. "Let there be no jungle"; & there was no jungle. He razed the earth with excavators to make space for his creations. & He made the low-lying metal sheds & *maquis* disappear. & He cloaked the land in roseate dust. & a wind swept over the land like water. *& that was the first day.*

*

"Let the earth yield mangos & pineapples & bananas & fruit trees of every kind on earth that bear fruit with the seed in it." & He transformed the jungle & the dark loam of the land into plantations, as geometric as a French garden. & it was so. *& there was evening & there was morning.*

*

& "Let there be a church in the midst of this cleared wilderness that can seat 18,000 people in pews made of *Iroko* wood. & let there be a stained-glass panel of myself beside Jesus ascending to heaven." So He imported architects & builders from France & Israel & Lebanon — from *everywhere*, but Africa — & He sent for Italian marble columns & French

---

[1] *Houphouet-Boigny was the Baoulé chief of his ancestral village*

21

stained glass. & so the "Basilica of the Bush"[2] was built. & it was so. *& there was evening & there was morning, the third day.*

*

"Let the remains of my ancestral village & its palaver tree now reside behind palace walls & out of sight. & let the waters under the sky be gathered around this palace." & so He built a behemoth & furnished it with two gold-plated rams at the door, gilded furniture & hundreds of servants. & the waters that were gathered together, he called *artificial lakes.*

& it was so. "Let the boulevards of my kingdom be as grand as those of Paris. & let those boulevards swell with adoring throngs, who come to pay their respects to their founding father. & let the tourists follow the swagger of the sun to a twelve-storey hotel at the end of an eight-lane highway, to marvel at the city of my birth." *& there was evening and there was morning, the fourth day.*

*

"Let the lakes bring forth swarms of living creatures." So He delivered crocodiles & carnivorous turtles to populate the lakes. & it was so. & He blessed them, saying, "Be fruitful & multiply & fill the waters of these lakes so that I might be protected as the chief of Yamoussoukro. "Let the earth bring

---

[2] *Also known as* the *Basilique Notre-Dame de la Paix or Basilica of Our Lady Peace.*

forth chickens to sate these starving reptiles. *And there was evening and there was morning, the fifth day.*

*

Then "Let me find a caretaker to have dominion over the dragons of the sea. & may he be a native of our neighbour, Mali." & so He hired a man to keep vigil over the crocodiles as the crocodiles kept vigil over Their One & Only King. *And there was evening & there was morning, in all of its excess.*

*

Thus, His heaven on earth was finalized. *And He rested on the seventh day.* But who else would ever rest?

THE CROCODILE FEEDER

for Dicko Toki,
Yamoussoukro, Côte d'Ivoire, West Africa

> *A piece of wood may sit in the water many years,*
> *but it won't become a crocodile.*
>
> *~ Malian proverb*

i.

a palace ascends from ochre earth, its artificial lake
ornate with imported reptiles:
leathery sentries that have weathered millennia,
meteorites, extinction

the crocodiles scull from the shallows with checkered tails,
shearing their path to an embankment
sullied by blood; a seething phalanx
inhaling feathered angst

pharaonic, they amass like an avalanche
of uprooted trees with thistled claws
and olive-streaked backs,
their pale underbellies pebbled yellow

their eyes see the world brambled with veins,
mouths emit an oily gleam;
their rocky hides and tides of teeth
tear the lair of men's dreams

ii.

At Ramadan's end, riveted tourists scrum
above sawdust banks, anticipating crimson

& rubbled bone, their cellphones ready
for the daily feeding ritual. Dicko,

the caretaker, plucks a bill from impatient fingers
& descends to the strand, a machete tucked

under one arm, a dingy chicken under the other.
Each squawk punctures the postmeridian torpor.

Rows of obsidian eyes vein the lake's drab skin.
Dicko swings the hen twice by its legs

wings frantic in the pitiless light. A trill
soaks the air amid shutter clicks.

Glutted, the crocodiles doze as Dicko tugs
one by the tail for the thousandth time & poses.

He taps the twisted snout of *Commandant*
& skips over the last of the reptiles

when the hem of his *boubou* snags in its jaw.
He trips over its tail, machete flailing,

stabbing the air as *Capitaine* drags him away.
Onlookers shriek, their eyes drown in jaws,

opaque with want. But no sound from Dicko.
No wail wedged between waves & stained teeth

as the beasts fissure water and sun, sinking
into a lake, reflecting nothing

and no one.

AU ZOO D'ABIDJAN / AT THE ABIDJAN ZOO

"When men were fighting over the last baguettes of bread in the shops, there was nothing to eat for the animals of the zoo, especially the carnivores who paid a heavy price during this crisis."

~ Kané Samouka, Directeur, Zoo National d'Abidjan on the effect of the post-election crisis on the animals.

"On ne demande pas à un homme qui a faim si son chien a mangé."

("We do not ask a man who is hungry if his dog has eaten.")

~ Proverb

I. STILL LIFE WITH ANIMALS

a savage heat / cloaks the forest
& the sick dusk /brings no relief

no longer / a derelict zoo
but a still life

where gunshots pulverize
the sky / & wreathe
this concrete prison

where feces & blackwater
clog dens

melancholy pervades
like tear gas /
aged trees sag / each cage is
an unfinished stanza

//

audible waves / of famine
in their bellies / serpents stir
in verdant heaps / & monkeys scratch
their bald heads / as they flay
blackening banana peels

still life /
        but for how long?

  //

the Iroko trees are cadavers
& at dusk / they are rubied
like hacked tusks

the antiqued eyes / of rifles
flame / between branches

these cages / hold
thin light
       & little else

II. LIONS' LAMENT

for Léa, Simba & Loulou

We were stabled in a scorched mosaic of smoke & fire, while another story blazed beyond the gates. Gone the splendour of our manes, mangy & matted, laurels of sorrow slanting over irises cloudy with want. Gone golden musculature, now disheveled sacks, the fretwork of bone shredding flesh.

We sank to our haunches, limbs crackling beneath us like kindling, too weak to whittle down the bars with our jaws. We hallucinated antelopes ripening at sunset, scarlet racks of meat, glinting pools of water.

O, how we envied the spider drifting between bars, toward the greening spires of the forest, toward the high nucleus of midday sun, unseen from where we sat, in the stench of our own unbecoming.

Hunger tames, but starvation slays. To live beyond our bodies, to wither, to wane. This is what betrayal tastes like: tawny grit of dust, gunpowder, torched tires searing our throats.

Abundance exists only in the larvae ripening in pungent air.

Near the end, we fed on the diminishing dark & the syllables of birds, in this citadel we would never leave.

A tire hung from a rope: a garrote, a gaping mouth & beyond that sightless eye, we saw the zoo wardens as good as hogtied. The need for forgiveness, pressed like a blade, against their throats.

III. THE LIONESS' PRAYER

for Lala

O my brothers, I beat my paws against your chests, stubbled with mud.

If only you could reap fire from my still-beating heart.

Let me be the hero for once — sidekick become sagacious apex.

Hear me even as the roar dwindles in your ears.

See me even as your retinas tear like the *savane*'s summer grasses.

Speak to me even as your throats are caked with dust.

Sweep away the bright eggs of maggots.

Drown out the drawn-out breaths of your brothers.

Do not yield to the black beast of hunger.

Do not sleep without dreaming.

Gorge on what's left of this life, what's left of the light.

IV. ODE TO TWO HYENAS

for Tomy & Tito

Stunted heads plunge
into carcasses, backs
spackled black. & an
unmistakable chortle

ejects from apish mouths.
Yellowing eyeteeth
& slather dangle
from sibilant maws

during this symphony
of feasting and vocalizing.
Follow the hyena's bumpy,
phonetic map: they blather

in glottal stops & consonant
clicks. A higher pitch
for fear & softer grunts
for cubs. A rallying whoop

for feeding & giggles
on a loop for any ruckus.

& don't forget the growling
vowels & timbre

of their almost-syllables.
A cackle has its glossary
for survival; their argot
supports their bravado.

V. ELEPHANT MEMORY

for CAN, the only forest elephant at the Zoo National d'Abidjan

In the absence of food, feed on memory:
feet sinking into the silken peat
of the waterhole, hush of mud-seamed faces,
plump tongues glued to the mineral lick,
elliptical ears flapping like fronds.

In the absence of space, forage
for that fragment of wildwood
unfolding slow as October sun,
its knotted tendons of liana
& acacia, sinewed & silvering.

Unyoke yourself from this loneliness,
whose spectral body flattens you
like the harmattan.

Feast on the veined earth
in all its communion:
from its termite skeins
to the deer's honeyed limbs,
from every smoking copse
to the osprey's blond oculus.

Imbibe the dreambody
of your father
& the mildewed soul
of your mother —
find refuge there.

Or perish.

VI. THE WARDEN'S EVENING CONTEMPLATION

The between-work
of the living
is knowing we are,
all of us,
made of longing.

And all our deaths
are as enmeshed
as any understory.

What is this knowing,
if not love?

SISSI BARRA: THE WAY OF SMOKE

San-Pédro, Côte d'Ivoire

*after the photography project, Sissi Barra ("Smoke Work")
by Joana Choumali*

In the morning, you are white as mercy, brown as a bittern's
wing, gray as goats' breath after rain. In the dusk, you are
crimson as a coxcomb, blue as a whetstone, black as a shovel at
day's end. You knuckle me like a right hook; each eye a
lozenge, weeping ash. You scissor my appetite. My heart is a
shard getting darker and darker.

//

I was born in the *Bardot* dust, not far from the barking sea. I
played in sawdust squalls, and on scabbed logs crisscrossing
the sewage. When I was eight, my mother took me to the
sawmill dump. The men sat in the warehouse while we picked
through the dregs — trashwood, treebarks, coconut shells. We
hitched a ride home and rigged the charcoal oven. A whip of
smoke curled like an *agouti*'s tail. The fire bucked, a darkling
mare, its mane a hammerfall of flames. The oven bawled, its
tears blessing the blueing wood. A day later, its slow and
beaten scent smouldered to prayer. Together, we broke the
oven open and collected its ebony trinkets with grateful palms.

//

Ashes hail a frail parchment. I shove through smoke's first lather, the fields shrieking its stench. Charcoal stubs poke through dunes like blunt snouts. I skitter across cinders. The heat a lit wick hitting me again and again. Sweat caramelizes my neck. A cough corkscrews my chest, my lungs sardined of air. The rain welts my body as my mother watches from the eaves. At night, I sink like an anvil into the mud.

//

A colony of bones unfurls, your clawed hands brushing my ribs. But I keep working. Because all my potential lives within your darkness.

//

Charcoal is a crop like any other. I stockpile patience. I work for a pittance. My tithe measured in the drenched hours, in San Pédro starlight.

//

I gather you in my arms, skin stippled white, sprigs of hair still damp. I clean your body with seawater, chant psalms into the seashell curl of your ear, bury you under the *bana* tree. I offer fresh water, kola nuts, millet flour and saliva so you may ascend to your ancestors. My half-winged daughter, I invoke the smoke to accompany you.

//

How do I dispel the night's viscera? By naming the invisible.
Her name was *Lolo*: star.

//

We billow in the ovens' afterglow, in that breach between
darkness and deed. Our shadows, supple as spiders, swim
through the air. As we breathe, we are eaten by smoke. A slow
cleaving of soul from body, so we may vanish one day into a
light taller than trees.

//

Widowed by smoke, we must find our own way. We sow
wings of ash upon our backs.

GRAND BASSAM SAUDADE

for the victims of the Grand Bassam terrorist attack & the people of Grand Bassam

after Joana Choumali's exhibit, "Ça va aller, a series of iPhone photographs printed on cotton canvas, and hand-embroidered.

this silence / is like
a shroud

I do not / know how
to unstitch it / nor do I
wish to

it keeps / the unsayable
intact / needled
together

//

each word / pearls
on my tongue
like water
over stone

no one / can yank
the skein / of sorrow
from my mouth

//

how do I   helm   this ship   home
     when   the last   hymn
     I hear   is the sea's
     metal slurry?

//

was the ocean / light or dark?

did a bullet stray / between waves
to unmake / another life?

did the sun die / in the water / that day?

//

only memory
has a voice
which percolates
through walls
of brine & longing

//

what's left / is the numb sky —
a stretch / of leaden sediment —
this beach still stained
with waves unspooling
into nothingness
riddled with filaments
of algae / like loose threads

//

all of night is grief's province
ever-generous, giving of itself
endlessly, no peace,
but an endless debris
of memories

night unsheathes my eyes
monsters forth its orphan chant
whets the edge between
the living & the dead

//

I   am   tethered   to   this   town

that	mends	itself		again	&	again
with	tendrils	of		seaweed	&	
knotted		rock		this		is
my		foothold		though		I
scramble		to	stay			

                                                                afloat

//

that day still lives / in me,
but I will let / the loom
of colour / thread / through

//

the sun proceeds/ loosens
itself from the ruins /swims
toward the darkness

the waves / over
each unstitched loop
like a mouth / widening
into speech

III

BRUSHED AWAKE

UNSOLICITED
PRESS
PORTLAND, OREGON
EST 2012

SELF-PORTRAIT IN METAMORPHOSIS

"There are four thousand muscles in a caterpillar./ It uses every one of them / to become something other than itself. ..."

–Matthew Olzman

I am a fatted candle
with fraying wicks
at both ends, sagging
with the burden
of flight on my back

Bound & burled
in this fleecy shroud,
almost bridal
in my creation

My world is without
aperture, I twitch
under the sun's nicks
& the prodding
of curious insects

The night is
made of static

& infinitesimal
pinpricks

the thaw begins,
its crimson blur —
to whir me
off the ground:

Pry me open & peer in,
see how I rewire myself:
my bristles become a lustrous jelly,
& my twelve ornamental eyes
learn something
of economy.

Nothing is expendable.

A chorus of muscle
dissolves into a horizon note
raucous with birds.

Even as I inch my way
toward mothdom,
the me that swallowed loam,
that corkscrewed
through orchards,
still exists.

Let the brine,
like tears,
imbricate me

I barely recall
the agony of forming,
the rigour of inhabiting
so many lives.

MAQUIS

Abidjan, Côte d'Ivoire

the belly of this hardscrabble street growls under bald acacia
trees. smoke from the cooking fires uncoils from metal roofs,
riddled with bird shit. in front, the floodlit disarray of rickety
chairs and tables, sticky with *bissap.* bottomless bass of the
radio rumbles, static bumbles from the football game.

a rooster's scabbed feet dart between plastic tablecloths. an
untethered dog yaps, taps its stumpy tail, skinny strings of
saliva swinging from jowl to jowl.

a woman hovers over the grill. wrists darken with the spatter
of palm oil and the gasp of chilis, her fingernails rap iron. the
air seethes with diesel, raw onion, singed feathers.

her thoughts simmer in dusk's orange silo.

the calabash spits, a runny yolk hisses. she jabs an eggplant
with a blunt knife. her fingers palpate braised catfish. she splits
gray snails from their shells with a hammer. flies wreathe her
nose, mouth. dull pearls of *attieke* crumble in a plastic bag.

evening brims with the blather of hungry customers. blond
globules of ginger beer blister red straws, young throats.
truckers loll, quaff *Drogbas,* trawling for *gos.*

she untwines one memory, and then another; they brine in the
swelter.

kids giggle, trip in and out of the shadows, spindly as
seedlings. night ferments. smear of cloud, scratch of stars.

she emerges, serves lukewarm plates. her head-wrap
unswaddles as she gnashes through the flak of dust and bug,
the din candling her nerves.

a baby bulges in the small of her back, eyes shuttered
against the fat moon.

Notes:
maquis: outdoor eating area in Côte d'Ivoire; also means "scrub" or "bush"
bissap: juice made of dried hibiscus leaves, sugar and mint
attieke side dish prepared from fermented cassava pulp.
Drogba: the beer "Bock de Solibra' is nicknamed "Drogba" after the celebrated,
Ivoirian footballer.
gos: young women

ODE TO SECOND MOTHERS

for the women of Amepouh, Abidjan, Côte d'Ivoire

you who mothered me   from loneliness when
others became dust   when husbands   ran far

& fathers even farther   when sisters recoiled
& gossips   uncoiled   their tongues

you   who saw me   as more than
a dowry   more than   dirty   blood

more than   a being   defiled by god
more   than a   death sentence

you   who led me   to the kitchen   & ate
from   the same plate   who cradled me

during my night sweats   who   shaped
my disease into   a word   I could speak

you who took   me   to my first screening
who bathed me   when no one else would

who trailed   a wet cloth   down my
gnarled vertebrae   & my skin stippled red

you   who mapped my hunger   & slumber
in the small hours   who kept vigil   under

the veiled stars   like the mother   I never had

mothers against   elegies & eulogies
requiems & exorcisms   dirges   & laments

mothers who devour loss like lions beautiful
& brazen   stalking death   to its lair

mothers   who gave me   my life   back
mothers   who gave me   back   to the family

that hated me   that forgave me

how can I ever   praise you   enough
for this alchemy   that wrings light   from dark

how do you render   such tenderness
where   there is   none?

BREAK/THROUGH

"And see how the flesh grows back / across a wound, with a great vehemence, / more strong than the simple, untested surface before."

– *Jane Hirshfield, What Binds Us*

Call it unlovely,
a wanton blotch,
an undone stitch

Call it the reef's
clamour seething
to the surface

a scorched line,
heat clawing its way
out of my body

Call it reptilian, a mottled seam
or a raw blossom
garish as a flare

Call it my
skin's frayed hymn,
my body's scripture

of what remains,
the gnarled root of memory
raking its debris
with metal teeth,

What dark wounds
we are made of.

I eulogize my skin
but I will never disown this —
revision, souvenir, script,
seal? — this gilded asymmetry,
of what was.

We heal ragged
even on the inside, pain inlaid
like an everlasting nacre.
Still

praise what was salvaged:
the self, ravaged
now rising.

LINGUISTICS

i.

out slips   sideways   the jabber
        of translation
        threadbare

sounds rumble   through
        the tunnel   of   my mouth
&   give up
                like a raven
stuck   in a
    drainpipe
i do   not   want   to
untell
            my   story   but
in this   impossible   drought,
        tongue   fattens
&   declares
                        mutiny
    upon   itself

inside   a silence   rides
        this   open   space   & sticks
binding   my   cry
                    like a burr
shall I quarry   this cavity?
    speech   like   pulling   teeth
        leaves   stumps
                red
        embedding me

in that   murky   cumulus
         of   leaving
even   my gestures
    grimace   & smirk
rooted   in   the gorge
        of   unknowing

ii.

where my elocution   was   confused   now   I   distinguish   a
clearing

mind   hopscotches   to & fro consonants knocking
against   each other

like   dropped bricks

mirror   words   but   they   come   out

     wild   widening   &   unwinding

like   a   faulty   parachute

    circle   the arena   of   conversation

& glitch   size   up   my   interlocutor

roll   each word   stillborn

marbling its rightness   then   soldier   on

sirening   its slang   into being

plucking   utterances   out of   this thrift shop

this linguistic swap   & blend

spun through   the snare   of   invention

relax   inside   this bracken   of   sound

braid   devotion   into   each   phrase

for there is   love   in   error:

how to create   a nest   out of   this poverty

of language   a map of sounds

that   is   hungry

to   expand   its   geography

iii.

Relief, like a stone-weight drops
& dissipates like rings into a well.

We have hammered out a dialect
from this faltering. Orient away

from reticence & toward outpour.
Brushed awake, the furrowed mind

turns over surfaces, new & old,

& fuses them together.

Sip the sweetness
of the spoken world.

iv.

Welcome to the voluble present, where rigour has been
muscled out of the guttural. We learn persuasion, debate, give
ourselves over to oration. My tongue is a cleverness of red.
When called, I steer words like a snake from its nest, all liquid
ease, speech greening from me in ribbons and radiating
beyond, gaining strength in meaning. No longer thirsty for a
system, double whole notes ladder up the canals of sound.
How does fluency taste — this arriving?

iv.

Underneath, we are,
each of us, raw with colour
like a tilled field.

Each cluster of stones articulates
a path, which mothers us
toward meaning.

Still, I will never unremember
those early days when I wondered:
who needs words?

When I looked at each foreign road,
graveled or blacktopped or dusty,
& thought: its muteness is real to me

LAUNDRYMAN HAIBUN

Attécoubé, Côte d'Ivoire

Hoist laundry on your head. Walk eight kilometres in the still-dark. Unravel on the riverbanks of Banco Forest. Glove hands in bags, thin as gauze. Herd garments to station — stack of sand-filled tires with slabs of rock atop. Soak each piece. Scrub with soap. Beat against stone. Soak. Scrub. Beat. Repeat. Soak. Scrub. Beat. Repeat. A woman glides along the river's spine, basin brimming with bricks of palm oil soap. Odour of soursop & potash floats from the steel drum. Reach for another brick. & another. & another.

hands sing over stone
sleeves of foam linger in the
river's greening mouth

A mob of *pagne* tinsels the river, the buttons like crushed ice. Fingers chafe, rough as jute. Gather wet clothes, wring & dry them. On grass. Or guard rails. Or the steel lattice, where odours of exhaust & trash overwhelm. Afternoon peters into evening. Tempers flare in air banal as cotton. You heat the iron over coals, press clothes & fold. Walk home in the brewing dark. Eat, sleep, wake. Repeat yesterday today. & tomorrow. & the day after.

shadows rise & fall:
pale replicas you shed like
this dawn-to-dark husk

O, meticulous men & women, who rise in dawn's hushed creases, still dreaming in their mother tongue, who weep soap until they breathe the gleaming edge of evening. O *Fanicos*, who never sleep, who keep dreams afloat for their sons & daughters.

the musk of marsh &
swill dissolves into your veins:
labour's sweet stench

EVENING

n. 1. the latter part of day and early part of the night. 2. the
period from sunset to bedtime. 3. any concluding or declining
period, as in / when the sun sinks below Ebrie lagoon / when
the boulangerie runs out of bread / when the boy wheels his
Nescafé cart with its one squeaky wheel / when drowsy babies
unfurl / on mothers' backs / at busy bus stops / when the first
flush of bats / darkens the sky / battering the clouds / to a
leathery pulp / fuchsia tongues tucked behind glittering teeth /
when monuments bow their heads / & weary prows list / when
mosquitoes jewel our ankles with blood / when the aftertaste
in the air is citronella & smog / when the musk from your
body / rises / warm & unmistakable / a scent swarming
everywhere / holding everything aloft / even the vagrant stars

~

UNSOLICITED
PRESS
PORTLAND, OREGON
SINCE 2012

FAT ODE

O blessed
be the prose of wood that blooms
the body's rose as such

O beautiful
the too-muchness of these statues
from head to burnished toe

O bountiful
circumference of ribboned wood
& every whorled skirt

O unabashed
surfeit of flesh blushing
beneath the carver's hand

O abundant
ballad of the rounded belly
& canticle of thick ankles

O eloquent
the speech of fat, of slackened arms
& thighs squat as turnips

O redolent
the brushed pinks & reds
of brazen mouths

O marvelous
all the more for the bold fractures
in their palm-oiled patina

O wondrous
contralto of robust goddesses, plucking
joy from the lyric dark

(exquisite shiver
of memory, how
you devour me.
When I see your uplifted
faces, by a thousand
cuts, am I freshly
slayed.)

ACKNOWLEDGEMENTS

I am grateful to the editors and readers of the following journals, in which these poems appeared, sometimes in an earlier form:

Best Canadian Poetry, 2018 & The Maynard: "Ode to the Cockroach"

Contemporary Verse 2: "Ode to Rust"

emerge 17, The Writer's Studio Anthology: "Abidjan Aubade"

The Ekphrastic Review: "Grand Bassam Saudade"

Eunoia: "Self-Portrait as Roundabout Mannequin", "Simulacrum", "linguistics" and "Self-Portrait in Metamorphosis".

The Fiddlehead: "atelier"

Okay Donkey: "break/through"

PULPLiterature: "The Chicken Carver"; "Laundryman Haibun"

The Learned Pig: "Le Président: Seven Days"; "The Crocodile Feeder"

Q/A Poetry: "red canvas"

Room Short Forms Contest, 1st place: "Sissi Barra: the way of smoke"

Radar Poetry, Finalist for *The Coniston Prize*: "Au Zoo d'Abidjan/At the Abidjan Zoo"; "Still Life with Animals"; "Lions' Lament" (*Best of the Net* nominee); "The Lioness' Prayer"; "Ode to Two Hyenas"; "Elephant Memory"; "The Warden's Evening Contemplation

Rust & Moth: "Four Aspects of Language [A sea lives on my tongue]"

SWWIM: "maquis"

Tinderbox Poetry Journal: "evening"

NOTES

"Elephant Memory": CAN was born on January 20, 1992, the day the Cote d'Ivoire's "Elephants" were victorious over Senegal in the 12th edition of the African Cup of Nations (CAN) football tournament. She survived the post-election crisis, but a few years later, succumbed to an illness.

"Grand Bassam Saudade" pays tribute to the 19 people killed and 33 people injured in a terrorist attack on March 13, 2016 in Grand Bassam, a city east of Abidjan. It is an ekphrastic poem inspired by Joana Choumali's *Ça va aller*, a series of iPhone photographs printed on cotton canvas and hand-embroidered. Choumali began the series one month after the attack as she observed the trauma that had overcome the city.

"Le Président": Houphouet-Boigny was the Baoulé chief of his ancestral village; Basilica of the Bush: Also known as the Basilique Notre-Dame de la Paix or Basilica of Our Lady Peace.

"Lions' Lament": The three lions died of starvation, despite the zoo wardens' best efforts to feed them during the post-election crisis. They are buried under the ancient trees near the zoo.

"The Lioness' Prayer": Lala, the Ethiopian lioness, died the day after the post-election crisis ended.

"Ode to Two Hyenas": Both hyenas survived the post-election crisis by feeding on rotten bread.

"Self-Portrait in Metamorphosis": The epigraph is from Mathew Olzmann's book "Build Now, A Monument" from his book "Contradictions in the Design".

ABOUT THE AUTHOR

Cara Waterfall is an Ottawa-born, Côte d'Ivoire-based poet, storyteller and mentor who teaches other writers how to sustain thriving, creative practices and reclaim their artistic identities. Her work frequently navigates the complexities of identity, place and intergenerational memory. She has post-graduate diplomas in Poetry & Lyric Discourse from SFU's The Writer's Studio, where she was mentored by Vancouver Poet Laureate, Fiona Tinwei Lam, and from the London School of Journalism. Her poems have appeared widely, including *Best Canadian Poetry*, *SWWIM* and *The Night Heron Barks*. She won *PULPLiterature*'s 2023 Magpie Award for Poetry, *Room*'s 2018 Short Forms and 2020 Poetry Contests. She is a three-time finalist for *Radar Poetry's* The Coniston Prize and was shortlisted for the CBC Poetry Prize. Her debut poetry collection, *Radiant Wound*, is forthcoming from *Unsolicited Press* in May 2025, and explores her life in Abidjan after the second civil war. She recently finished her second poetry manuscript, *The Lost Stations*, and is working on a third about *Nouchi*, a hybrid language that unites crucial threads of Côte d'Ivoire's identity. Subscribe to Cara's Substack, *Archipel*, an ongoing dialogue between poets and creatives of all kinds, celebrating the ways we connect through mentorship, community and transitions, launching summer 2024. www.carawaterfall.com

ABOUT THE PRESS

Unsolicited Press is based out of Portland, Oregon and focuses on the works of the unsung and underrepresented. As a womxn-owned, all-volunteer small publisher that doesn't worry about profits as much as championing exceptional literature, we have the privilege of partnering with authors skirting the fringes of the lit world. We've worked with emerging and award-winning authors such as Amy Shimshon-Santo, Laura Gaddis, Elisa Carlsen, Tara Stillions Whitehead, Heather Lang-Cassera and Anne Leigh Parrish.

Learn more at unsolicitedpress.com. Find us on Instagram, X, Facebook, Pinterest, Bsky, Threads, YouTube, and LinkedIn. Unsolicited Press also writes a snarky newsletter on Substack.